David Gl

Gas Lighting

A caricature of 1809 by Thomas Rowlandson. The woman on the right is a prostitute complaining that gas lighting could ruin her business. A number of similar cartoons were published to discourage the spread of gas lighting.

Shire Publications

CONTENTS

ACKNOWLEDGEMENTS
Photographs are acknowledged as follows: Castle Cary Museum and Preservation Society, page 12; Crown Copyright, Science Museum, London, pages 16 (left), 17 (top left), 21 (bottom left), 29 (bottom left); A. Marrack, page 17 (top right); Somerset County Record Office, page 9.

Cover: *A wall light of the early twentieth century.*

British Library Cataloguing in Publication Data: Gledhill, David, 1927-. Gas Lighting. – 2nd ed.– (Shire Album; no.65). 1. Gas-lighting – Great Britain – History. I. Title. 621.3'24'0941. ISBN 0 7478 0394 3.

Published in 1999 by Shire Publications Ltd, Cromwell House, Church Street, Princes Risborough, Buckinghamshire HP27 9AA, UK. (Website: www.shirebooks.co.uk)
Copyright © 1981 and 1999 by David Gledhill. First published 1981; reprinted 1987. Second edition 1999. Shire Album 65. ISBN 0 7478 0394 3.
David Gledhill is hereby identified as the author of this work in accordance with Section 77 of the Copyright, Designs and Patents Act 1988.

Printed in Great Britain by CIT Printing Services Ltd, Press Buildings, Merlins Bridge, Haverfordwest, Pembrokeshire SA61 1XF.

Typical inverted-mantle wall-bracket lights of the 1930s. The left-hand lamp is 14 inches (356 mm) in overall height, the other 7¹/₂ inches (191 mm).

EARLY EXPERIMENTS

It is not known who discovered gas, or who was the first to use it for illumination, but a number of men were experimenting with the idea of making gas from various substances during the seventeenth century.

The first man in Europe to record such experiments was Thomas Shirley, who in 1659 investigated gas that was bubbling up through the water in a ditch near Wigan. The Reverend John Clayton, who was the Rector of Crofton near Wakefield, in 1684 also investigated this source of gas and collected quantities of it in ox bladders, afterwards lighting the gas by applying a candle to holes pricked in the bladders. He also manufactured gas from coal taken from a seam adjacent to the ditch and, having kept this coal gas in bladders for some time, found it useful to 'divert strangers and friends' by setting light to it in the same way.

In 1727 Dr Stephen Hales experimented with Newcastle coal to produce coal gas, and in 1767 Dr Richard Watson, later Bishop of Llandaff, took these experiments further in attempting to purify the gas manufactured from pit coal.

Sir James Lowther in 1733 reported to the Royal Society on the 'damp air in a coal pit' belonging to him near Whitehaven in Cumbria, and in 1765 Carlisle Spedding, the colliery manager, used this supply of 'fire damp' from the mine to light his offices in Whitehaven. It is suggested also that he offered to light the streets of Whitehaven with this gas, but unfortunately the offer was not taken up. This appears to have been the only attempt at commercial exploitation of the idea of gas lighting during this period, although a German scientist named Diller gave displays of 'philosophical fireworks' at the Lyceum Theatre in 1788. The type of gas he used on this occasion is not known, but it is doubtful that it was coal gas.

In addition to these people who experimented with burning gas for illumination, one man, a Mr Barber of Nuneaton, proposed in 1791 to manufacture gas in a retort from 'coal, wood, oil or any other combustible matter' and use the gas produced for motive power – the foundation of what we know today as the internal combustion engine.

Right: *A large (diameter 13 inches, 330 mm) six-mantle ventilating light. These lamps were flued to outside (often via a convenient chimney) and so increased the amount of room ventilation. This is a twentieth-century version of a design popular in the mid nineteenth century for large buildings.*

Below: *An upright mantle wall bracket with comet shade.*

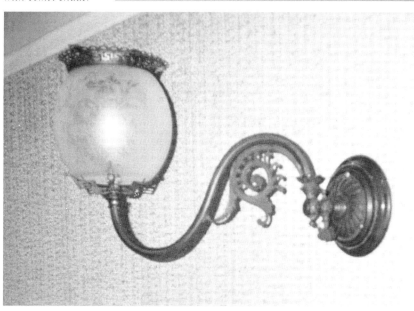

4

Typical two-light chandelier of the early 1900s.

THE PIONEERS OF GAS LIGHTING

Three men – John Pierre Minkelers, a Dutchman, Philippe Lebon, a Frenchman, and an Englishman, George Dixon – have a claim to have been the first to use gas for commercial lighting.

Minkelers was Professor of Philosophy at the University of Louvain, and in 1783 he produced a coal gas which he used to light his lecture room at the university. Philippe Lebon, a mechanical engineer, in 1796 produced a gas by heating sawdust. He wished to exploit his idea to the extent of lighting a part of Paris with this gas, but the suggestion was never carried through as it was overtaken by coal gas.

George Dixon used coal gas to illuminate his house in Cockfield, County Durham, in about 1780. Dixon was a colliery owner who sold some of his coal in the form of coal tar. During the process of extracting the tar from the coal he discovered coal gas, which could be used for illumination. His first experiments were with coals in an old tea kettle set in the fire, and he ran piping around two sides of his room by luting together tobacco pipes with clay. When gas was being produced by the kettle acting as a crude retort, it would issue from the end of the furthest pipe and would be lit. He would then make small holes with a pin through the clay that luted the pipe heads and shanks together, applying the flame of a candle to these holes so that there were as many flames in the room as there were pipe heads. On one occasion he attempted to extinguish the flame by striking it with his hat; this caused the gas to flash back along the tubes and an explosion occurred.

In a similar manner Lord Dundonald in 1787 lit Culross Abbey with gas obtained from distilling coal tar, but it is to William Murdoch, a Scot who worked in Cornwall and later Birmingham, to whom most people attribute the credit for the commercial exploitation of coal gas as a lighting medium.

William Murdoch experimented with a number of alternative fuels, and he also made coal gas by putting coal in a kettle and fitting a pipe to the spout. On one occasion, we are told, he reduced the end of the pipe by fitting an old thimble. The

5

thimble was worn and had a number of holes in the end, and hence was born the burner known as the flame retention head, a device which is still used to prevent the flashback of the flame along the gas pipe, which had caused the problems for George Dixon a few years earlier. In 1792 Murdoch successfully lit his house and office in Redruth, Cornwall, where he was employed as the senior engine builder for the Birmingham firm of Boulton and Watt. He also lit a street lamp outside his home by this method. The gas was produced in 'an iron retort', which he built in a yard next to the property in Redruth, and it was conducted into his building through tinned copper and iron tubes. Gas was said to be 'washed with water – and other means were employed to purify it'. Murdoch also collected gas in vessels and bags of tinned iron and leather or varnished silk to make a portable lamp, which he used to light his way around Redruth.

In the 1790s he left Redruth to be appointed manager of the Birmingham factory of Boulton and Watt, and he continued to experiment with gas-manufacturing plant, eventually building a plant that was used to light the Soho Works of the company in 1803. The following year Boulton and Watt sold their first gas lighting plant to George Lee, the principal of the cotton-spinning firm of Phillips and Lee at Salford, near Manchester. This plant was originally commissioned to operate fifty lights, and Murdoch reported thankfully that there was an absence of the 'Soho stink', which had been noted during his previous attempts. But the gasmaking apparatus was extremely crude, the retorts carbonised the coal badly, and the gas produced was neither washed nor purified. William Murdoch's satisfaction at the absence of a nasty smell must have been somewhat optimistic.

Nevertheless, despite the deficiencies of this gas lighting system, it was apparently regarded very highly by the purchaser, whose lighting costs were much reduced, as was also the fire risk. The installation was extended over the next three years until it served the whole factory, a short stretch of private road and George Lee's private residence, using 271 Argand burners and 633 Cockspur lights. These had the light equivalent of 2500 tallow candles, the relative costs being stated as about £600 per annum for gas and £2200 to £3000 for candles.

Independently of Murdoch, the idea of gas lighting was being demonstrated by Frederick Albert Winsor, an entrepreneur of German origin, who pursued the idea that gas should be manufactured centrally and distributed to the place where it was used, rather than being manufactured on the premises. Whilst Murdoch was undoubtedly a brilliant mechanical engineer and his assistant and eventual rival Samuel Clegg an experienced chemical engineer, Winsor had no engineering capacity whatever, a point which was repeatedly demonstrated by the ridiculous statements he made. Such was the lack of general engineering knowledge at the time, however, that these statements were believed, and his lack of engineering expertise did not cause him undue embarrassment. He was, moreover, a businessman of considerable enterprise, and it was he who gathered together the political and financial organisation necessary to make gas manufacture and its application to gas lighting possible in London by forming in 1807 the National Light and Heat Company, later, in 1812, given its charter and renamed the Gas Light and Coke Company, under which name it grew to be the largest gas company in the world.

Winsor first demonstrated gas lighting in London in 1807 and was responsible for the first gas street lights in Pall Mall later in the same year.

In 1814 the oil lamps in the parish of St Margaret, Westminster, were discontinued in favour of gas and crowds of curious people followed the lamplighters on their rounds. A year later there were 15 miles (24 km) of gas main in London and by the end of 1815 this had grown to 26 miles (42 km).

Winsor's first mains were made in lead by bending sheet lead around a mandrel, the longitudinal joint being soldered, but later mains were in cast iron. The cast-iron mains appear to have been satisfactory, even though they were often cast in a bore of as little as $3/4$ inch (19 mm) and with sides of unequal thickness, but this was not so with the pipes that took the gas from the main into the various buildings. These were often referred to as the 'barrel', a term which was used because the pipe was made in the same way as the cheap gun barrels of that period, namely a 4 foot (1.22 metre) length of strip iron bent over a mandrel and welded down its joint. Indeed, for cheapness, old or rejected gun barrels were often used as these were in ample supply during the nineteenth century, there being spare capacity in the armaments industry after the end of the wars with France.

Some illustrations of gas light fittings from a book published in 1815.

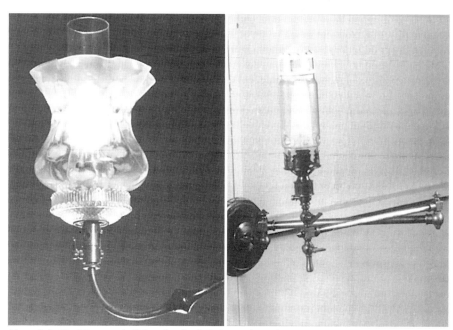

Above left: *Upright-mantle light. The shade is in vaseline glass, popular in Victorian times.*
Above right: *Upright-mantle wall-bracket light, with folding arm. The porcelain cap is to prevent marking of the ceiling above the light.*

Below: *A wall light in blue glass with brass fittings from the mid-Victorian period. The gas jet is puttied into the glass bracket. One of a pair over the fireplace in the Good Earth Restaurant, Wells, Somerset.*

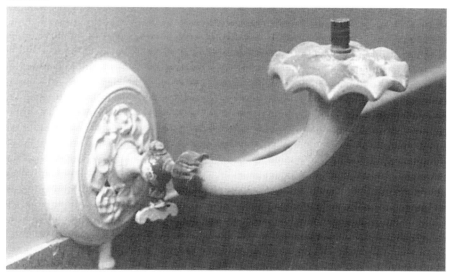

CREWKERNE GAS AND COKE WORKS.

PRICE OF LIGHTS PER ANNUM.

Description of Burners.	To burn from dusk until 9 o'Clock.			Ditto until 10 o'Clock.			Ditto until 11 o'Clock.			Ditto until 12 o'Clock.		
	£	s.	d.	£	s.	d.	£	s.	d.	£	s.	d.
10 hole Argand	3	0	0	3	10	0	4	0	0	4	10	0
12 do. Ditto	3	10	0	4	0	0	4	10	0	5	5	0
15 do. Ditto	4	5	0	4	15	0	5	5	0	6	0	0

If burned on Sunday, one-sixth to be paid in addition to the above.

The price above stated, is calculated for the flame not to exceed 4 inches; which being burned higher causes a waste of Gas, without any increase of light. Cylindrical Glasses are recommended to be used in preference to others, from their preserving an uniformly steady flame.

One Jet for Hall or Passage £1 15s. 0d. per Annum, until 11 o'Clock.
Bat's Wing Burner charged the same as the 12 hole Argand.
Gas by measure 15s. per thousand cubic feet.

The Rents to be collected quarterly, on the first day of April, July, October and January, and if not paid within one month after application made by the Collector, the service pipe will be cut off. The fittings to be done at the expense of the Consumer, and executed by a workman authorized by the Proprietors,

BRYAN, HOWDEN & COMPANY,

Engineers, Iron Merchants, and Manufacturers of Gas Apparatus,

40, *Bankside, Southwark, London, and Maidstone, Kent.*

Typical contract charges for the supply of gas.

THE COST OF GAS IN THE NINETEENTH CENTURY

Meters were not used for costing the gas supplied to consumers until the 1830s, and even then their reliability was much in doubt. Gas was often charged not by volume but by the number of burners in use for a given time – an arrangement which led to a great many inaccuracies, particularly as the gas was supplied at varying pressures dependent upon the amount being used at that time. (It could even drop to nothing and become extinguished at times of peak loading.) Also there was no standard as to the type of burner which should be used. Indeed, some people simply lit the gas at the open end of a pipe, making no attempt to use a recognised form of burner.

The first gas supply by the Gas Light and Coke Company was to seven consumers in the Westminster area of London in 1813. These consumers entered into a contract with the company based on the number of lights to be used in their premises, and the contract specified that gas was to be used only between dusk and 10 or 11 p.m. The use of gas outside these hours was prohibited, as also was the use of gas on a Sunday, although an exception was made in one case where lights could be used on a Sunday for an additional charge of 6 shillings. (This household's annual bill for lighting was £109 10s 0d.) This charge for Sunday use was usually one sixth of the daily contract rate, but some Scottish companies charged a higher price for gas consumed on Sunday by a 'burner that profaned the Sabbath by its light'.

In the early nineteenth century gas was still a very expensive commodity, out of the reach of the vast majority of people. Competition, however, was intense, and by the 1830s the price had been reduced in London from 16 shillings at the beginning of the century to 4 shillings per thousand cubic feet. By the end of the century the average price of gas had fallen to 2s 6d per thousand cubic feet, but the cost of lighting was still a large item in the average budget. The annual cost of providing a glimmer of light in one or two rooms in a house was roughly equal to one week's average wage.

By 1823 three rival chartered companies were operating in London, each invading the territory of the other, so that duplication of mains in streets was extensive, and it was not unknown for new supplies to be connected to the gas main of a rival company. Meters had not at this time been introduced, and therefore to prevent 'surreptitious burning' of gas on unmetered supplies (the use of gas light outside the hours of the contract) the practice was adopted of turning off the mains from sunrise to sunset. This was accepted by the gas consumer of that time, the only complaint being that gas lighting was not available for use on foggy days or dark afternoons.

In the 1830s gas stoves began to appear, and these created problems for the gas companies as they required a supply of gas during the day, when it was normally turned off. So the first of a number of 'day mains' were laid to supply consumers through a meter during the hours outside those specified in contracts. Whilst the day main apparently overcame the problem of the unmetered supplies it did not prevent the practice of connecting the new consumer to the mains of a rival company.

An ingenious method of discovering these frauds was practised by some gas company inspectors. It was known as 'jumping the lights'. The inspector would enter the house of a consumer known to be on the company's books and blow into the gas supply pipe, so creating a surge of pressure in the main outside. Meanwhile, a lookout (often a boy) was watching another house in the same street suspected of being connected to the same (but wrong) main, and if the lights in the suspected house were seen to jump up and down it was proof that one gas company was supplying the gas while another was being paid for it.

About this time, the main competitors to coal gas were the companies that sold whale oil for lighting, and these at first combined against the gas companies, claiming that mains gas was dangerous, poisonous – or a defiance of Almighty God. They were persuaded in the early nineteenth century to change their policy, becoming genuine competitors of coal gas by supplying gas made from animal fats and oils. This was manufactured through heated cast-iron retorts, but when the cast iron became covered with carbon they ceased to work effectively. When this problem became obvious the competition began to fail, and all the oil gas companies had ceased trading by the 1830s.

Competition from alternative fuels was not the only obstacle to be overcome in this period. In 1809 a parliamentary committee had told William Murdoch that obtaining light without using a wick was inconceivable. Indeed, when gas lighting was introduced into the House of Commons in 1852, MPs often placed gloved hands on the gas supply pipes in the corridors for fear that their temperature would become excessive.

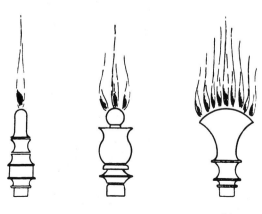

Rat-tail, Cockspur and Cockscomb burners of about 1808.

10

EARLY GAS LIGHT BURNERS

The first burners, as we have seen, were merely either holes in the pipes carrying gas or apertures left when the ends of pipes were partly blocked. The holes were often located so that the flame had a specific shape, and thus the Rat-tail, the Cockspur and the Cockscomb evolved. But it soon became fashionable to use ornate fittings for gas lighting, though even here the single or multiple jet was a method used for burning the gas.

The Argand burner had been used by the oil lighting industry for a number of years although its popularity had been somewhat restricted by its high cost. In 1809, however, Clegg was the first to adapt the Argand burner for use with gas.

The Argand burner works on a simple principle. It produces a circular rather than flat flame and introduces air for combustion both inside and outside the circle of flame. This results in better combustion and consequently an increased light output. It also usually included a glass chimney (necessary for burning oil), which helped to improve the combustion of the gas in those times when gas pressures were often variable and inadequate. From 1820 onwards the Argand burner was the main alternative to the simple jet, continuing until the introduction of electricity in the 1880s.

The single-jet type of burner was also improved, and the Batswing and Fishtail burners were introduced around 1816 and 1820. These resulted from the discovery that when two single jets were caused to impinge on each other an increase in the light output was achieved, and hence the flat flame jet was born.

A number of devices were introduced to improve further the simple jet. Probably the most important was the use by William Sugg in about 1858 of a non-metallic material, steatite, for the production of the tip of the jet.

At this time attention was also being given to controlling and regulating the gas pressure, and William Sugg was a pioneer in producing a governor-burner that could burn the gas at a constant pressure to maintain a good flame shape.

About the middle of the nineteenth century George Bray introduced his flat flame burners, taking the size from the usual maximum of sixteen candles up to eighty candles capacity.

In 1874 Sugg introduced the famous Christiania burner, which proved extremely popular at the end of the nineteenth century, often being made with ornate (and sometimes gold-plated) metalwork supporting beautiful white (Albatrine) shades. These shades were sometimes in cut glass but often had coloured scenes painted on them by French artists.

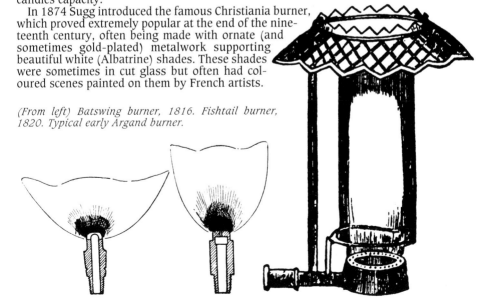

(From left) Batswing burner, 1816. Fishtail burner, 1820. Typical early Argand burner.

A pair of early wall lights made of buffalo horns; from a butcher's shop in rural Somerset.

During the last quarter of the nineteenth century meters had been introduced so that gas could be charged more reliably, and the problems of varying gas pressures had been solved by the introduction of governors, not only on the burners, but also at the gasworks. The gas was therefore being provided clean, at a consistent quality and at constant pressure.

GAS FOR PUBLIC ILLUMINATIONS

Throughout the Victorian period public illuminations were a popular means of celebrating national or local events, and gas lighting was frequently used to provide an appropriate display. As early as 1802 William Murdoch had celebrated the coming of peace by arranging an exhibition of gas lighting on the wall of the premises of Boulton and Watt in Birmingham.

During Victorian times the usual procedure was to form appropriate figures with a multiplicity of small lights, either single jets or small burners complete with shades, which prevented the lights from being blown out. Usually the shapes were made in wrought-iron pipe and the jets formed by drilling holes in the pipe approximately 6 inches (150 mm) apart. The shapes were typical of Victorian England and often made direct reference to Queen Victoria herself.

A coloured flare was often included. The colours were produced by adding various chemicals to the gas as it was burnt in an open dish. These flares had flames that could be up to 3 feet (1 metre) high.

THE ARGAND BURNER

A measured uniformity was now called for in the amount of light, and the Argand burner was chosen as the standard by the City of London Gas Act of 1868.

The Argand burner was made in a variety of sizes in late Victorian times, probably the largest being one with four concentric steatite rings and designed to have a lighting value equal to twelve hundred candles. At this time it was common for manufacturers to offer gas lights with either the flat flame jet or the Argand burner.

The last quarter of the nineteenth century was a time of great social change and much scientific innovation. Lighting both in the house and in the street had become essential and, as the price of gas was still high, ways were sought to increase the lighting output of the various burners available. One such idea was the regenerative lamp, which was introduced in 1886 to apply the principle of preheating the combustion air from the heat contained in the flueways of the light.

Another idea for increasing the efficiency of gas lighting was the Albo-Carbon light, which used compressed naphthalene in the form of sticks or balls to increase the light output of the coal gas. With this device, after a flat flame burner had been operating for several minutes, the light became much brighter and the illuminating power was increased from 10 to 30 candle power.

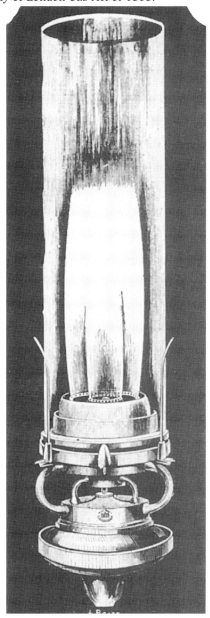

Right: Argand governor-burner with two rings of flame.

Below: A design for a Victorian public gas illumination.

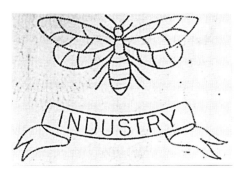

13

THE INCANDESCENT MANTLE

The invention of the incandescent mantle allowed gas lighting to continue its growth and popularity into the twentieth century – until the competition from electricity took effect. Two men were responsible for this innovation: R. W. Bunsen, whose name is still used to define the traditional aerated burner, which was a development of the Argand burner of that time; and Carl Auer von Welsbach, who is credited with the invention of the incandescent mantle. These two developments were contemporary with each other, however.

The appearance of electric light in the 1870s provided the incentive for research into the improvement of gas lighting by other means than simply relying on the incandescence of the carbon content of the coal gas flame. Investigations initially took the form of suspending solid bodies in the gas flame with the idea of obtaining light by the incandescence of these bodies, and hence was evolved the incandescent mantle, which revolutionised gas lighting.

In 1862 Jouvet patented a gas burner that had a small metal cap, the edge of which was to be raised to incandescence by a Bunsen flame, and four years later J. A. Hogg invented a similar burner that had a mantle made of platinum 'or some other suitable refractory material'.

Edison in 1878 proposed coating the platinum wire with the oxides of zirconium and cerium, and in 1880 Wenham (who earlier had invented the recuperative lamp) constructed 'a cage of very fine platinum wire to enclose the Bunsen flame, but knowing that thin platinum in time becomes disintegrated, brushed on a protective coating, consisting of a paste of very fine fluorspar'. By this means he obtained a brilliant light from otherwise invisible flame.

Two other people made important progress towards the incandescent mantle. The first was Lewis, who in 1881 patented an incandescent burner, which included a mantle of platinum wire gauze. These mantles yielded an excellent light when new but quickly deteriorated with use, giving an illuminating value of about two hundred candles for a gas consumption of 40 cubic feet per hour.

The following year a Frenchman, Clamond, exhibited at the Crystal Palace a mantle which consisted of a conical basket composed of threads of calcined magnesia. At its best efficiency the Clamond burner and mantle gave four candles per cubic foot of gas consumed, but the chief drawback was the comparatively short life of the magnesium basket, which burned out in about one hundred hours. Both these designs were discussed in detail in an article in *The Times* in 1882.

In the United States in 1881 Haddon proposed that strands of platinum and iridium should be placed horizontally over a naked flame, and in 1883 Fahnehjelm, a Swedish chemist, proposed to suspend 'threads or rods of refractory material for the production of light by their incandescence' over a gas flame. These yielded three to four candles per cubic foot of gas consumed per hour but, as with previous ideas, they were not commercially successful because of the short life of the rods.

In the 1880s von Welsbach effected a great improvement in gas lighting. He discovered and patented the possibility of making an incandescent mantle using chemical rather than metallic substances. His method was to manufacture a mantle that would fit around a Bunsen flame in cotton fibre, and this in turn would form the medium to support the chemical substances which would produce an incandescent light. The cotton was, in fact, burned away before the light was put into operation. This new invention was given a great deal of publicity in the London press, although one authority who viewed the exhibition of this 'new gas light' in 1887 was very critical of its flimsiness.

In 1887, however, the Incandescent Gas Light Company was formed, and the first factory to produce gas mantles was opened in Westminster. The price of the burner at this time was one guinea and the mantle 5 shillings. It was also necessary to take the burner back to the factory in order to have a new mantle fixed to it. This was

Far left: *Jouvet burner, 1862.*

Left: *Clamond incandescent lamp of 1891.*

quite a problem as it was reported that in transmitting a small parcel of mantles from Westminster to a consumer in Ipswich, 'although they were carried with every possible care, half of them were found to be broken by the time they reached journey's end'.

Shortly afterwards the company found itself in difficulties and was reconstructed, and by 1890 this problem had been solved. The first Welsbach mantles were inferior to those which were produced after the reconstruction of the firm. Before 1889 it was considered satisfactory for the mantles to provide a light of six to eight candles per cubic foot of gas, but after the new company was formed this figure was increased to twenty candles per cubic foot.

The progress which incandescent gas lighting made in Britain is indicated by the rapid growth in the sale of burners. The number sold in 1893 was 20,000; in 1894 it was 105,000 and in 1895 300,000 were sold.

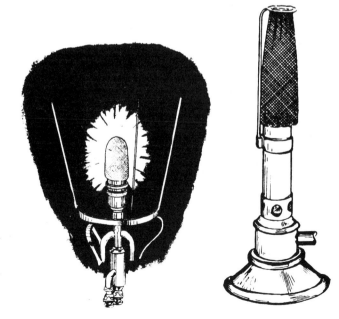

Right: *Lewis platinum mantle burner of 1883.*

Far right: *Von Welsbach's experimental burner and incandescent mantle, 1887.*

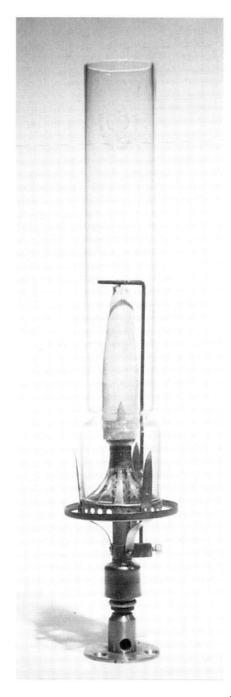

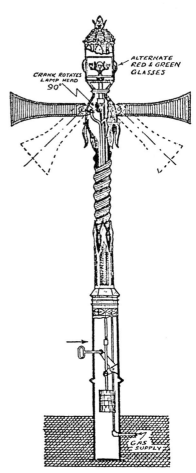

Above: *A rare example of a gas light used in a traffic signal. This gas-lit signal, described in 'The Times' of 9th December 1868, was installed in the middle of the road outside the Houses of Parliament to assist a policeman directing both road traffic and pedestrians crossing the road. Three gas jets were fixed at the top of a 20 foot (6.1 metre) post. The handle at the base would rotate the lantern through 90°, so controlling both road traffic and crossing pedestrians. Only red and green glasses were used, as this was considered adequate for horse-drawn vehicles. The trial ceased in 1872.*

Left: *MacTear's burner, 1887.*

Above left: *A fine example of a Wenham light with case in Doulton pottery. Increased illumination was obtained by the regenerative process.*

Above right: *An Albo-Carbon device with six gas jets.*

Below: *The Twi-light, an early example of the introduction of the mantle.*

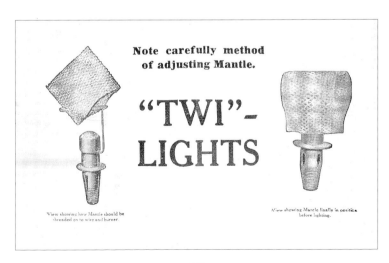

Note carefully method of adjusting Mantle.

"TWI"-LIGHTS

View showing how Mantle should be threaded on to wire and burner.

View showing Mantle finally in position before lighting.

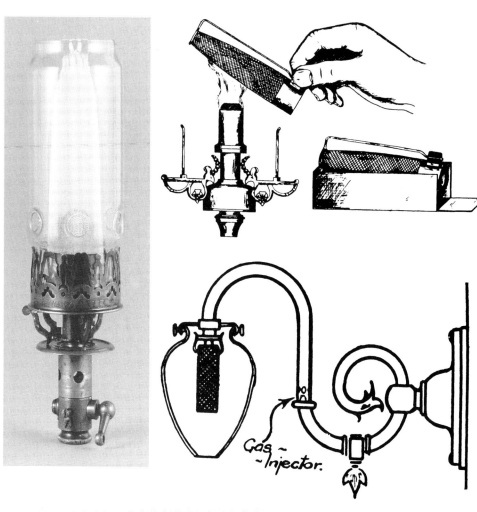

Top left: *'C' pattern burner introduced in 1893.*

Top right: *Heald's improved burner of 1889, showing 'burning off' of the mantle before use.*

Above: *Kent's inverted burner, 1897.*

Left: *Magna Midget incandescent mantle.*

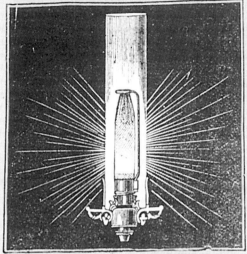
An advertisement dated 1890.

THE DEVELOPMENT OF THE INCANDESCENT GAS BURNER

The first burner manufactured and sold by the Welsbach company in 1887 was the invention of MacTear, the deputy chairman and technical adviser to the company, and it followed closely the original design used by Carl Auer von Welsbach.

In 1889 the Incandescent Gas Light Company introduced an improved gas burner, the invention of Arthur Heald, the improvements being: the burner was more ornamental than its predecessor; it was advertised to 'consume 2½ cubic feet per hour giving 25-30 candles illuminating effect'; adjustment of the gas consumption could be carried out by a small regulator in the base of the burner; and a new method of supporting the mantle by a rod passing up the centre of the burner had been introduced. Later the company introduced the C pattern burner in 1893, a model that was to be very popular for the next three decades.

The Welsbach upright mantle, however, did not have a monopoly of the market. In the 1890s it had a number of competitors, one of which was the Magna mantle. This was designed to improve the open jet type of lighting that was available up to that time. It was very simple and somewhat crude but increased the light output from flat flame jets with only a little additional expense or complication.

Even so, in the 1890s the Welsbach type of upright mantle was the best available and was the principal weapon used to combat the rising competition from electricity,

19

as advertisements of the period show.

About 1895 consideration was being given to a defect in the upright mantle design, namely that the burner itself produced a shadow at ground level, whereas this was not so at ceiling level. Consequently the inverted mantle, as we know it today, was born, and in 1897 Kent produced a gas mantle burner which, it was claimed, gave 'a downward light free from shadows'.

It was possible to fire the gas flame downwards without the help of a boosting device only because the gas was being supplied to the consumer not only at a better quality but at an increased and more constant pressure than fifty years before. By this time a gas pressure of 2 or 3 inches (50-75 mm) water gauge was normal and could be relied upon, whereas in the middle of the nineteenth century the gas pressure varied from 0.7 inches (18 mm) water gauge at the best times of the day to virtually nil at times of maximum consumption.

Since the early years of the twentieth century Kent's basic design for an inverted burner has not changed except that the burners of around 1900 were made of brass or copper with porcelain and have since been superseded by the present simpler design made in aluminium and magnesia.

An advertisement in the 'Illustrated London News' of 1887.

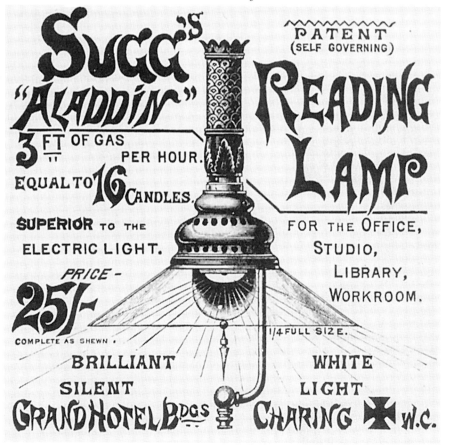

Left: Thistle jets with steatite tips, c.1880s.

Below left: Water slide gasolier (chandelier) with upright burners, about 1870. The water-filled telescope stem allows the height of the burner to be adjusted as required for different activities.

Below right: Type of ornamental gas fitting by Sugg in use about 1875.

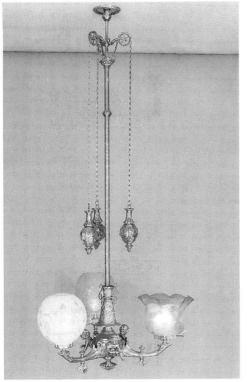

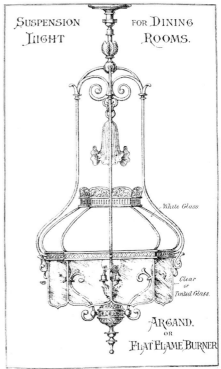

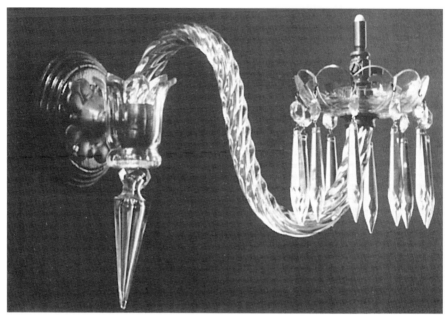

A cut-glass light bracket of Victorian times. These glass brackets were also fixed in groups of four or six on a centre pipe to create a gasolier (chandelier).

Some shades for Sugg's Christiania burners.

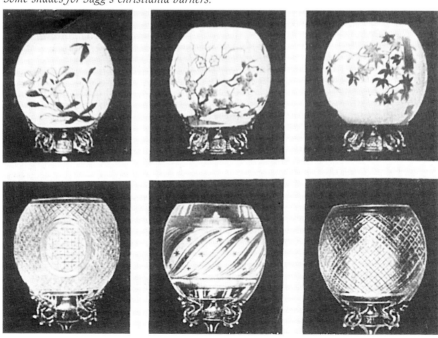

Above: *Illustrations from the 1912 catalogue of George Bray & Company Limited.*

Top right and bottom right: *Two examples of upright-mantle wall-bracket lights.*

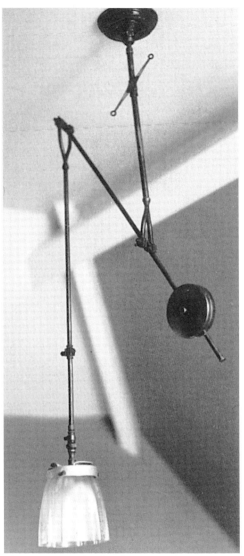

Above: *Gas 'anglepoise' lamp, popular in kitchens and some workshops in the 1930s.*

Left: *A selection of small wall lights dating from about 1900 to 1980. The centre bracket is fitted with a black-out shade from the Second World War. The shade is made in steel, painted black, and has a ring of holes in its base for the only emission of light. The lowest model is the most recent; it was produced for a few years when strikes in the coal industry made electricity supplies unreliable.*

Above left: *The Streatham pendant light, a lamp whose opaline shade is supported by a fitting in cast aluminium and pottery; twentieth century.*

Above right: *A later example of a butterfly wing burner in aluminium, with 1930s shade. The function of the disc over the light is to deflect the products of combustion and so avoid dirtying the ceiling.*

Left: *An early example of the inverted mantle, with cut-glass ruby shade and shell-type burner of pottery and copper. Two inverted-type mantles can be seen. These burners, dating from c.1905, were soon superseded by the cheaper model shown in the photograph above right.*

Original advertisement introducing the pneumatic gas switch.

SWITCHING AND IGNITION DEVICES

SWITCHING

It was the competition from electricity (which could be switched on so conveniently) during the late Victorian period that caused the introduction of gas switches as an alternative method to the conventional plug cock for turning on the gas manually.

The first was the pneumatic switch, which was introduced in 1903. This had a small copper tube that enabled the switch to operate a pneumatic valve fitted adjacent to the light, the tube being usually buried in the plaster of the wall and having a bore of approximately 1/16 inch (less than 2 mm).

In 1929 the Newbridge system of switching came into operation. This device consists of a gas cock operated by means of a Bowden wire from a switch that had either a vertical movement, as in today's electric switches, or a rotary movement. (The Bowden wire system is that which is used to operate the brakes of a bicycle.)

A third type of gas switch, the Webson, operated from a small electric battery which was housed in the bakelite case and which in turn operated a small electric valve fitted on the gas light.

Webson switch.

Pneumatic gas switches and the pneumatic valve.

Newbridge mechanical gas switches.

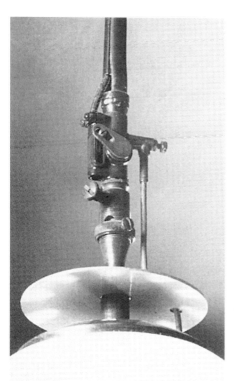

IGNITION

Ignition of the gas following switching was by one of two methods: either a permanent gas pilot or by causing a small electric element to glow adjacent to the gas mantle. The pneumatic switch relied upon a permanent pilot, but the Newbridge amd Webson range of switches would operate with either of these two methods of ignition.

The Newbridge Company also specialised in a range of hand-wound clockwork switches chiefly for use with street lighting, where the lamps were switched on and off automatically at predetermined times.

Left: *An example of automatic switching from the 1930s. Note how the Bowden cable, which turns on the gas, is fitted into a special groove in the gas supply pipe. Ignition is by permanent pilot.*

Below: *Newbridge mechanical switches with electric ignition facility.*

Right: *Table lamp, c.1920s, with cast-iron stand and inverted mantle.*

Below left: *Table lamp, c.1870s, with upright burner.*

Below right: *An early twentieth-century hall light.*

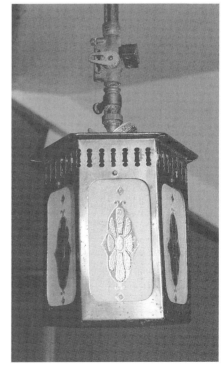

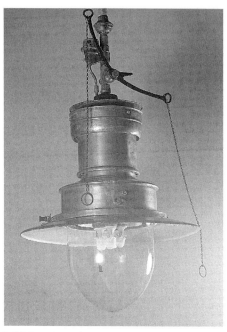

Above left: *A large copper outside lamp with three mantles. Typical of lamps used in railway stations in the twentieth century, this model is a Sugg's Rochester.*

Above right: *A large enamelled three-mantle lamp often fitted in school halls or similar buildings.*

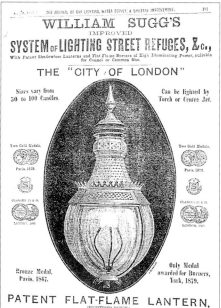

Left: *A nineteenth-century advertisement.*

30

FURTHER READING

Barty-King, Hugh. *New Flame.* Graphmitre, 1984. Especially recommended.

Chandler, D. *Outline of the History of Lighting by Gas.* South Metropolitan Gas Company, 1936.

Douglas, J. 'Albo-carbon', *Journal of Gas Lighting,* 22nd July 1879.

Griffiths, J. *The Third Man.* Deutsch, 1992.

Hunt, Charles. *A History of the Introduction of Gas Lighting.* Walter King, 1907.

Illustrated London News and Supplement, 14th December 1872. The gas strike in London.

Marrack, A. 'Albo-carbon', *The Midnight Oil,* number 30, summer 1998.

O'Dea, W.T. *The Social History of Lighting.* Routledge & Kegan Paul, 1960.

Tann, Jennifer. *The Development of the Factory* (pages 123-35). Cornmarket Press, 1970.

These two gas lights were fitted in a Somerset church in 1837. On the left is a large cast-iron bracket with five brass tubes and steel burner tips, each drilled with two small holes angled so that the flames impinge to produce a ragged luminous flame of irregular shape, about 3 inches (75 mm) high. Below is an early Argand gas light with a brass burner that would produce a ¹/₂ inch (12 mm) cylinder of luminous flame. The clear glass chimney is missing.

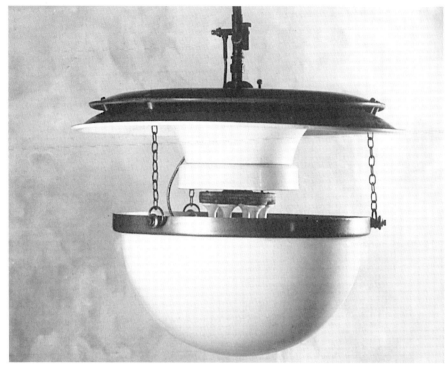

Named the Bon Marche lamp, the opal glass bowl was made in sizes up to 16 inches (406 mm) in diameter. This type became popular in the twentieth century.

PLACES TO VISIT

Intending visitors are advised to find out opening times before making a special journey.

Abbey House Museum, Abbey Road, Kirkstall, Leeds LS5 3EH. Telephone: 0113-275 5821.
Biggar Gasworks Museum, Biggar, South Lanarkshire. Telephone: 0131-225 7534.
Bradford Industrial Museum and Horses at Work, Moorside Road, Eccleshill, Bradford, West Yorkshire BD2 3HP. Telephone: 01274 631756.
Fakenham Museum of Gas and Local Industry, Hempton Road, Fakenham, Norfolk. Telephone: 01328 855579.
The John Doran Museum, Aylestone Road, Leicester LE2 7QH. Telephone: 0116-250 3190.
Museum of Science and Industry in Manchester, Liverpool Road, Castlefield, Manchester M3 4FP. Telephone: 0161-832 2244. The Gas Gallery.
Science Museum, Exhibition Road, South Kensington, London SW7 2DD. Telephone: 0171-938 8000. The Gas Gallery.
York Castle Museum, Eye of York, York YO1 9RY. Telephone: 01904 653611.